COLOR MY SENSES

Paula Aquilla BSc, OT, DOMP

Color My Senses
The Sensory Detective Coloring Book

All marketing and publishing rights guaranteed to and reserved by:

800-489-0727
www.sensoryworld.com
info@sensoryworld.com

ISBN: 978-1935567660

Dedication

This coloring book is dedicated to all the
sensational children and the parents and teachers
who support them!

We can taste. We can touch. We can see. We can do these things because we have a nervous system. Our nervous system sends information to our brain about what's happening in and around our body. It delivers information from our body to our brain and from our brain to our body. Every action of our body is controlled by our nervous system. This system is marvelous and works automatically; we don't even have to think about it!

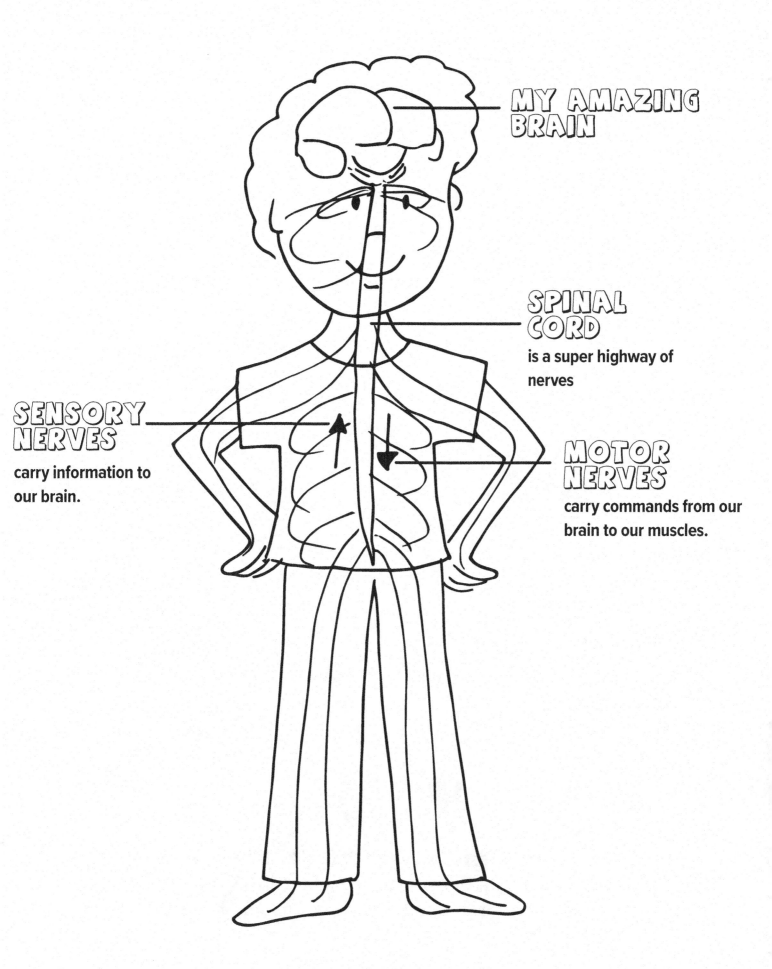

MY AMAZING BRAIN

SPINAL CORD
is a super highway of nerves

SENSORY NERVES
carry information to our brain.

MOTOR NERVES
carry commands from our brain to our muscles.

3

VISUAL
see the rainbow

PROPRIOCEPTION
feel the position of your
foot as it touches the
ground

VESTIBULAR
balance on one foot

We have a sense of taste, a sense of touch. These senses are part
of our sensory system. Our sensory system carries information from
our senses to our brain and tells us what is going on in our body and
in our environment.

INTEROCEPTION
feel your stomach growling

AUDITORY
hear the bird chirping

OLFACTORY
smell a good treat

GUSTATORY
taste the treat. Yum!

TACTILE
feel the cold water

The senses in our sensory system are vision, balance and motion, hearing, smell, taste, touch, and body awareness.

VISION

Let's use an example to explore the senses. Suppose we want to cross the road. We look both ways to make sure it's safe to cross. Oh! What's coming?

A school bus drives down the road and we watch it pass. Our eyes carry information about what we see. We use our vision to see the bus. Seeing happens in our VISUAL SYSTEM.

Our head can stay level so that our eyes can follow the bus. The sense of balance and motion (connected to our inner ear) carries information that helps us keep our head level and our posture upright and also keeps us from falling down.

We use information from our sense of balance and motion to stay on the sidewalk. Balancing and moving happens in our VESTIBULAR SYSTEM.

Semicircular canals inside
my ear help me rebalance

We know exactly how to move our head because our sense of body awareness gives us information about our body in relation to other people and objects. Our body awareness also tells us when we are close to the curb and the road so we can back up onto the sidewalk and be safe. We can even close our eyes and feel the position of our body! Body awareness happens in our PROPRIOCEPTION SYSTEM.

Close your eyes now...are you sitting or standing? Where are your hands? You just used your proprioception system to answer these questions!

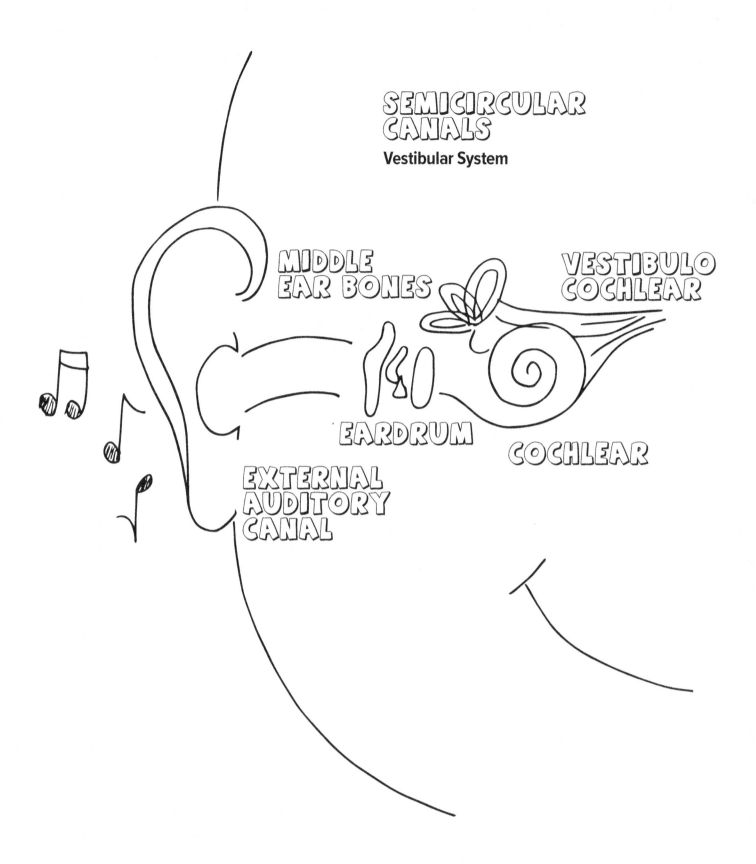

SEMICIRCULAR CANALS

Vestibular System

MIDDLE EAR BONES

VESTIBULO COCHLEAR

EARDRUM

COCHLEAR

EXTERNAL AUDITORY CANAL

The engine of the bus makes a low rumbling sound. Our ears carry information about what we hear. Hearing happens in our AUDITORY SYSTEM.

The exhaust from the bus smells stinky. Our nose carries information about what we smell. Smelling happens in our OLFACTORY SYSTEM.

Sometimes we can taste what we smell because our mouth works with our nose to give us information about what we taste. Tasting happens in our GUSTATORY SYSTEM.

As the bus roars past, the air pushes against our face and moves our hair. Our skin carries information about what we feel. Touch happens in our TACTILE SYSTEM.

Feeling hungry and wondering if we have any snacks in our bag shows our sense of internal body awareness at work. This system is called our interoception system. This system carries information from inside our body and gives us physical information about hunger, toilet needs, fatigue and temperature. Interoception also provides information about how we are feeling; our emotions and the intensity of those emotions. Internal body senses happen in the INTEROCEPTION SYSTEM.

Our sensory nerves bring sensory information to the brain stem, where we put all the information together like a sensory puzzle. Important sensory information is sent to the brain and the brain attaches meaning to the sensation. It is in the brain that meaning is given to what we experience.

Unimportant sensory information carried by our sensory nerves is disregarded. We can ignore the scratchy hat on our head or the baby crying behind us when we are crossing the street because it is not important to crossing the street. This is called SENSORY MODULATION. Sensory modulation also enables our brain to attach the correct meaning to the sensation we are experiencing.

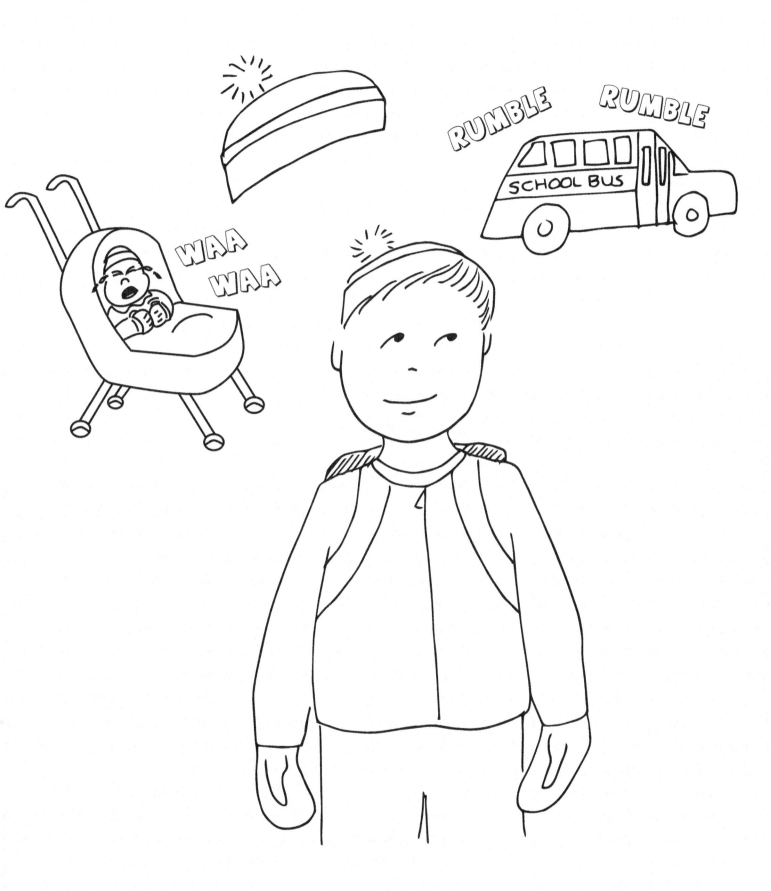

The sensory information sent to the brain must pass through the limbic system before it reaches the brain. The limbic system controls stimulation, emotions and memories.

If we are interested in what we are doing and motivated to complete the task, sensory information goes to the brain. Then meaning is given to the information: The bus has now passed; it is safe to cross the road.

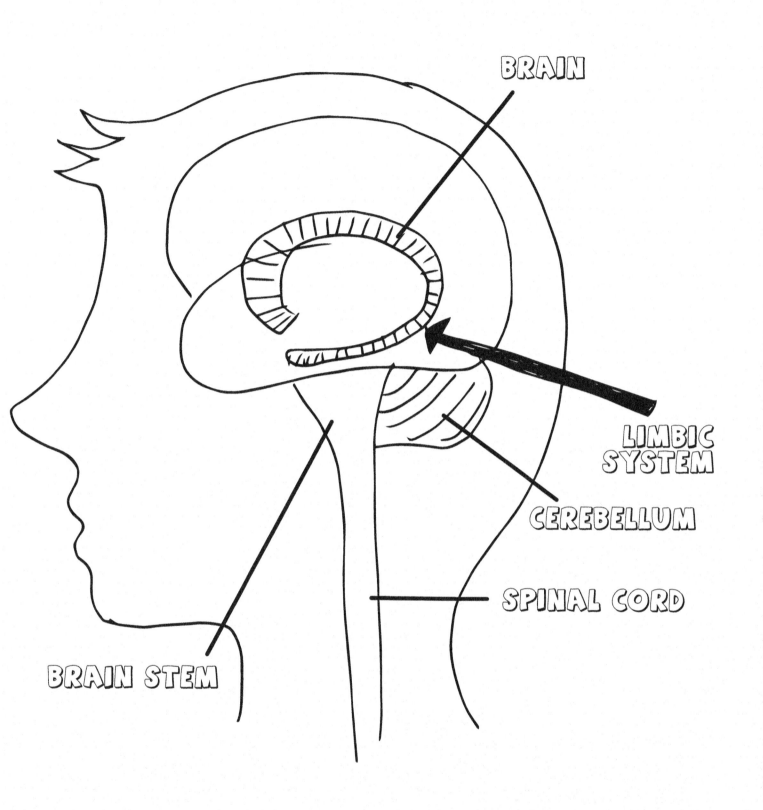

BRAIN

LIMBIC
SYSTEM

CEREBELLUM

SPINAL CORD

BRAIN STEM

BRAIN

SPINAL CORD
carries signals from
the brain to the
muscles

LEG MUSCLES

How does your body know to move? The brain tells the muscles to move
by communicating with the spinal cord muscles through motor nerves.
The messages from these nerves tell muscles when, how fast, and how
strongly they should contract so that the body moves forward and we can
cross the street. Motor messages from our brain to our muscles happen
in our motor system.

Our senses give our brain information constantly so we can change our movement and make it better. For example, if we see a car coming, we can walk faster or even run!

If our mom calls us, we can locate her with our eyes and say, "Hi, mom!"

Our sensory and motor nerves are always helping our brain talk to our body, and our body to talk to our brain. It is marvelous!

Paula Aquilla, B.Sc. O.T., D.O.M.P.

Paula Aquilla lives in Toronto with her husband Mark and daughters Katie and Ella. Paula is an occupational therapist (since 1986) and an osteopathic manual practitioner (since 2011). She works with adults and children in clinical, educational, home, and community-based settings. She founded the YES I CAN! INTEGRATED NURSERY SCHOOL, YES I CAN! SUMMER CAMP and the I LOVE MY BABY PROGRAM in Toronto and served as the director for six years. Paula was also the founding executive director of GIANT STEPS, a private school for children with autism, at the Toronto location. She runs a private practice serving children with special needs and their families. Paula has given many workshops on the use of sensory integration internationally. She created the occupational therapy program at Aptus Treatment Centers where she continues to consult. Her practice is an approved placement for students from the University of Toronto's occupational therapy department, where Paula is also a guest lecturer. She is a professor at the Canadian College of Osteopathy, and a consultant to the MacMaster University Occupational Therapy students. Paula is the proud co-author of **Building Bridges through Sensory Integration**, and **The Sensory Detective Curriculum**. She brings warmth, knowledge and enthusiasm to her work with children.

CPSIA information can be obtained at www.ICGtesting.com
Printed in the USA
BVOW04s0334051016

464200BV00004B/5/P

9 781935 567660